I don't care
if you like
my name or not.
That's my name.
It's the only
name I've got.

MY Book about ME

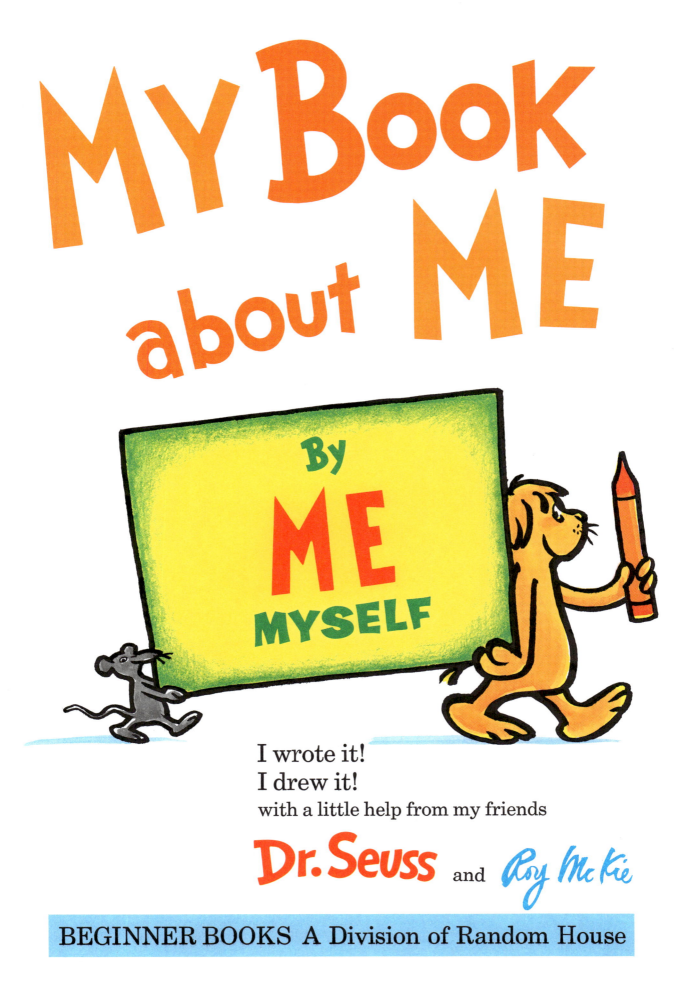

By
ME
MYSELF

I wrote it!
I drew it!
with a little help from my friends

Dr. Seuss and *Roy McKie*

BEGINNER BOOKS A Division of Random House

TM & copyright © 1969 by Dr. Seuss Enterprises, L.P.

All rights reserved.
Published in the United States by Random House Children's Books,
a division of Random House LLC, New York,
a Penguin Random House Company.

Random House and the colophon are registered trademarks of Random House LLC.

Visit us on the Web!
Seussville.com
randomhouse.com/kids

Educators and librarians, for a variety of teaching tools, visit us at
RHTeachersLibrarians.com

ISBN: 978-0-394-80093-6
Library of Congress Control Number: 75-85289

Printed in the United States of America
110 109 108 107 106 105 104 103 102

Random House Children's Books supports the First Amendment
and celebrates the right to read.

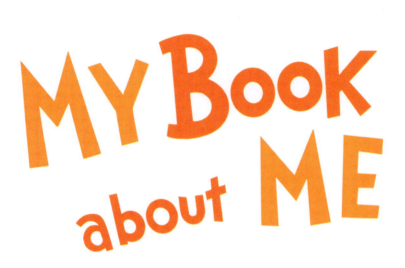

First of all

there is one thing
you should know.

Am I a boy?
Or am I a girl?

Well,
I'll tell you.

I am a
GIRl

I weigh ___43___ pounds.

How tall am I?

I am ___4___ feet,

___4___ inches tall.

My Teeth

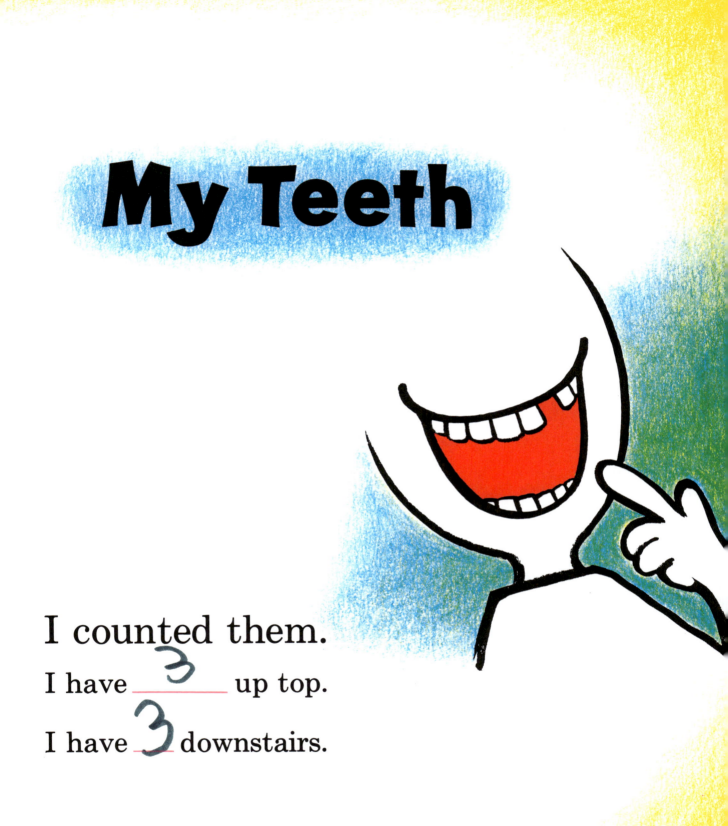

I counted them.
I have ___3___ up top.
I have 3 downstairs.

My Hair looks like this:

I drew it in.

Straight hair

Curly hair

Long hair

Short hair

Pony tail

Blonde hair

Black hair

Brown hair

Red hair

Orange hair

Purple hair

White hair

Gray hair

Green hair

No hair

My Hand is this big.

(I drew around it with a pencil.)

Do you want to know
how big **My Foot** is?

Well, this is how big.

(I drew around it with a pencil.)

Long nose

Short nose

Up nose

Down nose

Broken nose

My Nose

THIS is how my nose goes.

I drew it.

My Eyes

Blue eyes

Brown eyes

Green eyes

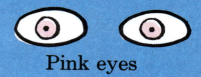
Black eyes

Pink eyes

Hazel eyes

Gray eyes

THIS is the color
of my eyes.

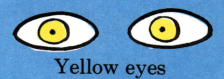
Yellow eyes

Eyeglasses

I wear glasses. ☐

Check one.

I don't wear glasses. ☑

10

FRECKLES

I don't wear freckles.

Check one.

I do wear freckles. ✓

I think I have about __1000__ freckles.

11

Where in the world do I live?

I live in one of these countries.

Afghanistan	Belgium	Central African Republic	Ecuador
Albania	Benin	Chad	Egypt
Algeria	Bermuda	Chile	El Salvador
Andorra	Bhutan	China	Ethiopia
Angola	Bolivia	Colombia	
Argentina	Bosnia and Herzegovina	Congo-Brazzaville	Fiji
Armenia	Botswana	Congo-Kinshasa	Finland
Australia	Brazil	Costa Rica	France
Austria	Bulgaria	Croatia	
	Burma	Cuba	Gabon
Bahamas	Burundi	Cyprus	Gambia
Bahrain		Czech Republic	Georgia
Bangladesh	Cambodia		Germany
Barbados	Cameroon	Denmark	Ghana
Belarus	Canada	Dominican Republic	

Haiti	Libya	Pakistan	Switzerland
Honduras	Liechtenstein	Panama	Syria
Hungary	Lithuania	Paraguay	
	Luxembourg	Peru	Taiwan
Iceland		Philippines	Tanzania
India	Macedonia	Poland	Thailand
Indonesia	**Madagascar**	**Portugal**	Togo
Iran	Malawi		Trinidad and Tobago
Iraq	Malaysia	Qatar	Tunisia
Ireland	Maldives		Turkey
Israel	Mali	Romania	
Italy	Malta	Russia	Uganda
Ivory Coast	Mauritania	Rwanda	Ukraine
	Mauritius		United Arab Emirates
Jamaica	Mexico	Samoa	United States
Japan	Monaco	San Marino	Uruguay
Jordan	Mongolia	Saudi Arabia	Uzbekistan
	Morocco	Senegal	
Kazakhstan	Mozambique	Serbia	Vatican City
Kenya		Sierra Leone	Venezuela
Korea (North)	Nepal	Singapore	Vietnam
Korea (South)	Netherlands	Slovakia	
Kuwait	New Zealand	Somalia	Yemen
	Nicaragua	South Africa	
Laos	Niger	Spain	Zambia
Latvia	Nigeria	Sri Lanka	Zimbabwe
Lebanon	Norway	Sudan	
Lesotho		Swaziland	
Liberia	Oman	Sweden	

I live in

If you want to send me a letter
here's my name and address.

If you want to phone me,
call this number:

7764 8 8 P

My House

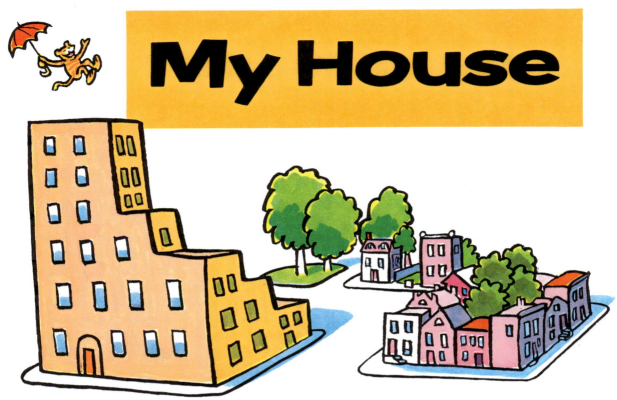

Apartment house

House in the city

House in a town

House in the country

House in the mountains

House in the desert

House in the suburbs

Farm house

House near the water

Igloo

The house I live in is:
Subrbs

My House

has _12_ windows.

My house has _3_ beds.

My house has _13_ pictures on the walls.

My house

has __13__ steps.

There are __11__ forks in my house

My house has

__2__ keyholes.

In my house, there are _____ lights.

We have ____4____ clocks.

In my house, there are _8_ mirrors.

We have _2_ cold water faucets and _2_ hot.

I eat like a horse.

I eat
like a bird.

I eat like a __bIRd.__

My favorite food is

and PeYSa aND

and I'S KReiMe

And please

don't give me any

BeTCHTPSe

I can't stand it.

My Birthday

is

Month ___JaNuary___

Day ___30___

Next year
I will have _7_ candles.

I drew in
the right number
of candles.

24

If you really want
to give me a
Birthday Present
here is what
I want most of all.

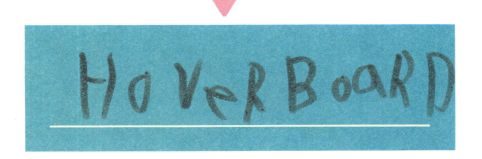

HOVERBOARD

Happy
Birthday
to ____

(But if it costs
too much,
forget it.)

I Go to School

I go on foot.

I go on my bike.

I go by helicopter.

I go by bus.

I go by car. ☑

I go by subway.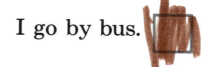

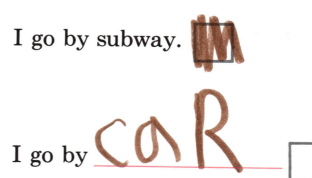

I go by caR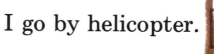

My favorite teacher's name is

HUGHES

Reading   Math

Spelling   Art

Writing

Music

I study many things.

I like WRiTing best.

I like MUSiC worst.

I am a very good student. ☐

I am a so-so student. ☑

I am awful. ☐

I have read about RFKCPP books.

My favorite book is _____

I am right handed. ☑

I am left handed.

I am both handed.

I can stand on my hands
for _____7_____ seconds.

My feet are ticklish

YES

NO ✓

Dog

Cat

Bird

Monkey

Alligator

Guinea Pig

My Favorite Pet

Fish

Pig

Hamster

Gerbil

Pony

Horse

Bear

Turtle

Donkey

Snake

Goat

Skunk

Mouse

Rat

Squirrel

Toad

Octopus

is Dog

Frog

Ants

Lizard

Lamb

I have one. ☐

I wish I did. ☐

Rabbit

Cow

Porcupine

Hippopotamus

Some Secret Things I Know

It is **20** steps
from my door
to the first tree.

It is ___8___ steps
from my tree
to the first mailbox.

It is ___1000___ steps
from my mailbox
to the first store.

I bet YOU never knew *that* before!

My Clothes

I own exactly ___3___ buttons.

And I counted my zippers.

I have ___10___ zippers.

My

Favorite Color

is

blue

My Very Special Autograph Collection

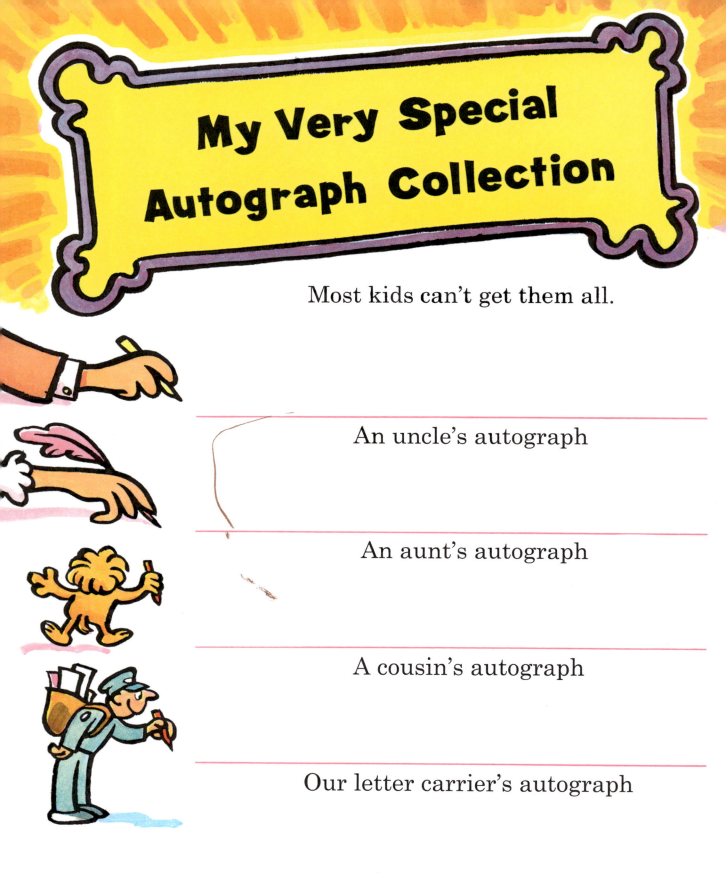

Most kids can't get them all.

An uncle's autograph

An aunt's autograph

A cousin's autograph

Our letter carrier's autograph

A grandmother's   A grandfather's

A firefighter's autograph

A grocer's autograph

POlIce

A police officer's autograph

A delivery person's autograph

Autograph of a man with a beard

Autograph of a man more than 6 feet 3 inches tall

My Best Friend is

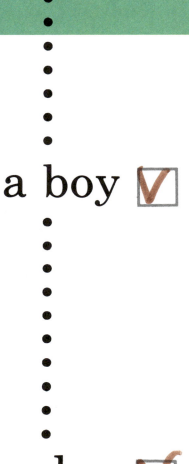

a boy ☑

a dog ☑

38

□ a cat

☑ a girl

My best friend's name is:

_____

Here is how to spell it backwards:

_____

Sometimes

I Get Mad at Some People

YES NO

Check one.

I kicked someone.

YES NO

I pushed someone.

I hit someone.

I yanked hair.

I'm sorry I did it.

My Longests

My longest walk was ___BRADBARe___ miles.

MoWtEMe

My longest bike ride was ___ay la___ miles.

My longest car trip
was ___takstse___ miles.

My longest plane trip.
___takstse___ miles.

42

My longest fish was
0 feet, *0* inches.

My longest swim was
0 miles, *0* feet.

My longest hair
is *8* inches.

I CAN DRAW
funny pictures
like this

I drew this bird

His name is _____Bad_____

My Hobbies

I collect

stamps

sea shells

birds' eggs

nothing

coins ☑

string ☑

butterflies ☐

walrus whiskers ☐

What else?

I collect _____

_____

My Favorite Sport is

SGeyNIN9

I am very good. ☑

I am sort of good. ☐

I am not so good. ☐

My Favorite Song is

K WE NOV MEN

I sing in my bath.

 YES NO

Check one.

I am a great whistler.

YES NO

I hum better
than I whistle.

YES NO

Guitar

Xylophone

Trumpet

Cello

Violin

Trombone

Drums

Piano

My Favorite
Musical Instrument
is

viola ho

Very neat

Not so neat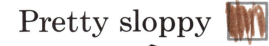

Pretty sloppy

I talk in my sleep.

I never talk in my sleep. ✓

I like to get up
at _____ o'clock.

I can make NOISES

like a rooster ☐

like a dog ☐

like a cat ☐

like a goat ☐

like a sheep ☐

like a goose ☐

like a train ☐

like a _____

like a _____

like a _____

My family loves
my noises.

| YES | NO |

Farmer	Plumber	Electrician	Cook
Doctor	Carpenter	Firefighter	Pilot
Nurse	Secretary	Police Officer	Writer

When I Grow Up, I Want to

Lion Tamer	Racecar Driver	Football Player
Truck Driver	Coach	Hairdresser
Astronaut	Frogman	Dress Designer
Mechanic	Painter	Mathematician
Violinist	Model	Stockbroker
Taxi Driver	Baseball Player	Movie Star
Minister	Computer Engineer	Photographer
Priest		Alligator Wrestler
Nun		
Editor		Horticulturist
Librarian		Paleontologist
Musician		Coal Miner
Burglar		Gold Miner
		Rabbi

Artist	Actor	Tailor	Teacher
Dentist	Banker	Soldier	Nothing
Letter Carrier	Lawyer	Sailor	Dancer

Be

Judge	Gardener	Millionaire
Jockey	Senator	Singer
Jeweler	General	Cartoonist
President	Butcher	Locksmith
Accountant	Sculptor	Blacksmith
Flight Attendant	Pianist	Salesperson
Mother	Acrobat	Shopkeeper
Father	Watchmaker	Zookeeper
Magician	Dog Trainer	Statistician
Mayor	Explorer	Veterinarian
Sea Captain	Manufacturer	Zymologist
Window Washer		Yak Trainer
Bus Driver		
Camel Driver		

I Like to Write Stories

Here is one I wrote.

_____

_____

_____

_____

_____

_____

_____

_____

_____

_____

_____

_____

_____

_____

_____

Good story, isn't it?

Well, sir! That's MY Book About ME.

I finished writing it

_____ Month

_____ Day

_____ Year

HI!

I'm back again.

Here are three things about Me

I forgot to tell you.